AD
D
LIB
ERATION

ALSO BY SAI MURRAY:

Kill Myself Now: The True Confessions of an Advertising Genius
(Peepal Tree Press, 2008)
Co-Editor: *No Condition Is Permanent: 19 Poets on Climate Justice and Change*
(Platform, 2010).
Editor: *Re-Membering: A Creative Journey to Wholeness* (AiM, 2010)
Editor: *The Write Stuff* #1,2,3 (AiM 2009-2012).

AD-LIBERATION

SAI MURRAY

PEEPAL TREE

First published in Great Britain in 2013
Peepal Tree Press Ltd
17 King's Avenue
Leeds LS6 1QS
UK

ISBN 13: 9781845232061

Supported using public funding by
ARTS COUNCIL
ENGLAND

ACKNOWLEDGEMENTS:

Versions of some of these poems have been featured in the following publications or exhibitions:

SABLE: Black British Perspectives; *Scarf mag* #3: Breathing Space (Numbi); *Popshot* magazine #4: The Modern Living Issue; *Red: Contemporary Black British Poetry* (Peepal Tree); *No Condition Is Permanent* (Platform); Gallery artwork at The Arnolfini; *The Write Stuff* #1 ('Artists in Mind); *Creative Freedom: The FWords Anthology* (Peepal Tree); *Abeng Soundings: Abolitionist Landmarks of Our Freedom-march* (S2007B); *Going Down Swinging* (GDS Magazine); *Dance The Guns to Silence: 100 Poems for Ken Saro-Wiwa* (Flipped Eye); *A Lime Jewel: Anthology of Poetry and Short Stories in aid of Haiti* (Black Londoner Appeal); *The Hat You Wear* (The Manchester Independent Book Market); *Cartographies of Justice* (Liverpool Hope University); *Human Rights Consortium Poetry Anthology* (The University of London).

With thanks to:

Kadija George, Dorothea Smartt and the Inscribe family for the continued nurturing and beginnings; Jeremy Poynting and Kwame Dawes for their kind and true scalpelling; 'Don' Jacob Ross and all at Peepal Tree Press; Jane Trowell and the Platform family for continued support and inspiration; Virtual Migrants for the motivational mash-ups; John Holt and Artists in Mind; Kinsi Abdulleh and the Scarf team for the Afropolitan Numbi niceness; Zena Edwards and the Shake! family; Leeds Young Authors; Esther Stanford-Xoesi, Kofi Mawukofi Klu and the extended Global Justice Forum family for continued groundings; to Caroline, Reuben, and all other family.

For Dad,

Fatherhood

and any sane mad-men.

CONTENTS

V

GENESIS

This first reading is taken from the Gospel of Genius,
Chapter 1, Verse 1:

In the beginning was the word.
The word made flesh.
The word sold flesh.
Good-looking, sweet-smelling,
smooth-sounding, fantastic feeling,
fresh, new, tasty-fresh flesh.

In the end there is only the word:
A. Alpha. Aaaah.   Advertising.

Advertising is art.
The greatest most rewarding
most creative of all professions.
Advertising is not work.
Advertising is life: an attitude,
a way of life, the Life.

To do the art justice you need to
live, eat, drink
and breeeeathe it.
Deep.

Advertising is an art form
that consumes the artist;
an art form requiring the artist
to consume all other art forms.
In this sense it is the highest art form.

From Gauguin to graffiti;
Guggenheim to ghetto;
Mozart to Mos Def;
independent indigenous doc
to Hollywood block;

Malcolm X to Xtra-strength mints
to X-box to Generation-X to X-Factor
to not giving a flying X-rated XXXX.
Xcetera, Xcetera.

Fact: advertising is better than art.
Advertising = art plus language.
A plus B... lartguage... langart... advart?

The perfect combination of communication.
The image + the word.
The image + the word
+ the sound + the taste
+ the smell + the feel.

Advertising is all.
A. Alpha. Aaaah.   Advertising.

For thine is the kingdom,
the power and the glory,
forever and ever,

Adman.

WHITE ACCENT

Around the time that some Saro-Wiwa fella is front page news
we sit, summoned, at the back of big chief's office. Junior free-

lancers, on placement, placed together (well we do have the
same skin tone) to give us both a better chance of breaking in.

The campaign is for a sticky amber soft-drink, one that we can
only dream of getting our magic markers on. Senior copywriter

number one recalls the shoot up in Edinburgh. Apparently –
the funniest maddest thing right, was that this black guy, that

one driving the truck, he had the strongest Scottish accent – jackal
cackle rocks the room. Big chief, not creative director for nothing,

quick as a flash – *yeah but he was shit at doing a black accent wasn't*
he – bays of laughter. Sycophant symphony. We do not look at

each other, junior copywriter, junior art director, eyes ahead. For
now, our bleed-proof layout pads will stay blank on this one.

FAILURE

Had I not tried to kill my self, I would be famous.
A successful adman. Lots of awards, lots of sex,
lots of drugs, lots of money.

I would have graduated to TV, film, music, fashion.
Bigger awards. More sex, mo' drugs, mo' money.
Latest trends. Fast car, big house. All the gadgets.

I would have travelled and partied the world over.
Dating celebrities and super-models.
Many friends, many many girlfriends, one or two wives.

That was what I wanted, desired.
I had the skills, ambition, smile, charm.
Sure diggedy, that was what I would have got.

ad-liberation *noun*

1. the act or process of gaining freedom from the malignant influence of corporate advertising/ marketing.

2. process by which corporate employees attempt to atone for their destructive actions.

3. any attempt to counter the madness of consumer society.

I.

Advertising is the greatest art form of the twentieth century.

— Marshall McLuhan

I had expected to become Prime Minister when I grew up. Instead, I became an advertising agent on Madison Avenue; the revenues of my nineteen clients are now greater than the revenue of Her Majesty's Government.

— David Ogilvy,
Confessions of an Advertising Man

CAREER SUICIDES FOR THE CONSCIENTIOUS ADMAN

Choose death, choose trendspotting, choose to die
57 million varieties to try:

Choice of a generation – choke on a Coke
Indian water, no tonic, down throat.
Slit neck swiftly with sleek Silk Cut
Spill sticky tar quick – red oil slick.

Swim with a tiger shark in your tank
Send out no ESSO-S, no listening bank
Do not pass Ogoni. Straight to hell. Suffer sHell-shock
from pump-action petrol pistol – glock.

Draped in Emporio Armani – taunt the poor Rio army
Never mind the poverty Gap,
Stitch sweatshop sweat shirts till it hurts.
Heroin chic needle through skin, looking good, super-slim.

Prod eye with poison Apple i-Pod
Knock ear with a Nokia, knife knee with a Nike
Head butt glass-ceilinged Windows XP –nentially…
Not so Micro-soft.

An American Express-ion
Fall like stock from a trade centre
Lose your (bank) balance
Have A (multiple) Break: Kit Kat me-ow.

EA EA, oh bad sports
Old McDonalds has a factory farm
Live like a chicken nugget in a barn
Have a nice day, a Happy (last) Meal

Amen Mr Adman.

AA

My name is Simon.
I'm an adman.

I've been clean for several years.
It is thirteen years, nine months, three weeks, two days
since my last corporate ad campaign.

I am an addict. Brain damaged:
a permanent propensity for punnery,
a legacy of loquacious ad-libs.

With the help of family, friends and my sponsor,
I hope to control my ad-diction,
I shall try to resist the compulsion to relapse.

II.

art is the opposite of advertising
poetry makes love with the language
advertising rapes the language

— Adrian Mitchell

AN UNSUCCESSFUL GIG

Police are today conducting enquiries following a failed attempt to blow up a south London stage. The suspect is reported as a Black male, carrying a ruc-sac, and speaking with a strange northern accent – "the only funny thing about him" according to one disgruntled audience member. Authorities remain bemused as to how easily the suspect gained entrance to the venue, and managed to secure top billing as the final performer of the night. On approaching the stage, the would-be terrorist openly broadcast his desire to "raise the roof", "blow up the house", "blow open minds." His efforts in this respect proved distinctly amateur: lacking basic material for the task, his heavy mix of explosives failed to ignite. The potent concoction did, however, see one young audience member in close proximity to the stage, nod into unconsciousness. Several painful minutes ensued before the suspect finally imploded. No-one was seriously shaken by the blast. Police caution that this individual may still pose a threat to the wellbeing of the general public and although failing in his mission on this occasion, he did certainly bomb.

HUMBLED IN THE BACK OF A BROOKLYN TAXI

Somewhere between
the jubilation of performing our first New York gig
in front of two paying guests
and the reverie of an upstate library reading
in front of friends, family, strangers,
the taxi driver mentions that
he too is a poet

Somewhere between
the Jewish quarter with trench-coated men
patrolling the streets with beards, black hat UFO's
and submachine guns,
their women pushing prams
in the surreal twilight,
the taxi driver tells us
he was once on Def Poetry Jam

Somewhere between
our failed attempt to find a jazz club
and our much-needed beds
we find a bar
buy the taxi driver a drink
and the taxi driver drops a poem.
He thanks us.
We thank the taxi driver more.

@MODEM_LVNG_

@ModernLiving is   creating an account
(about 3 minutes ago)

@ModernLiving is   attempting to convey profound witty
oh-so-cool irony in < 140 characters

@ModernLiving is   tagging self in havin' it, happy, smiley,
what-an-oh-so-crayzee-life-I-lead photos

@ModernLiving is   deleting derogatory comments/un-
tagging incriminating, unflattering photos

@ModernLiving is   listening to, reading, watching, wearing,
copying, liking the latest craze #cray

@ModernLiving is   googling self, page 5 of about 146,000,000
results

@ModernLiving is   googling ex workmates, ex schoolmates, exes

@ModernLiving is   join/follow/friend/visit/add/watch/like/RT
my post, status, picture, group, page, blog,
site, vid, me. pls

@ModernLiving is   1,423 new friends, 562 followers,
56 notifications, 49 comments, 16 requests,
12 pokes, 2765 unanswered emails, 28 texts,
2 missed calls

@ModernLiving is   correcting the misinformed views and beliefs
of new friends

@ModernLiving is   ~~@#??/**!!!**EMOTIONAL!!!!!!!*
*\\$@:><

@ModernLiving is   regretting having posted when drunk/ angry/
                    emotional

@ModernLiving is   beginning to see, act, think
                    in < 140 character statements

@ModernLiving is   searching for sports results... gossip...
                    love... sex... pornography

@ModernLiving is   #bored.

@ModernLiving is   searching for a life

@ModernLiving is   in need of a holiday

@ModernLiving is   away from the desk

@ModernLiving is   out of the office

@ModernLiving   ...

@ModernLiving has deleted account
                        (1 second ago).

JACK MAPANJE LAUGHS AT LIZARD POO

The former political prisoner who has skipped without rope
in a sweating, scorpion-filled jail, covered in his own shit
to win a shower, sits yoda-like at the Tendaba camp bar.

It is our first night in the Gambia; for some our first time
in the Motherland. Away from the commotion, I join the
jovial poet for a beer and explain what all the fuss is about:

those small black raisins that we found in our rooms
turned out not to be raisins.

BROKEN VERSE

Through sweet marijuana whisps
A snake delivers to your door.
Or was it that skunk all along?
Red eyes, screw face, blurred vision.
For a second, I inhale too.

Exhale.

This divide and rule is nothing new.
Paranoia, pride, poverty.
We both know respect runs deep.
Shoulder to shoulder, stanza to stanza,
We battle. Roots intertwined.

The abeng calls our pens elsewhere.

III.

It is not the Black child's language that is in question,
it is not their language that is despised: it is their experience.

— James Baldwin

The truth is that marketing raises enormous ethical questions every
day – at least it does if you're doing it right. I would rather be thought
of as evil than useless.

— Rory Sutherland
President of the Institute of Practitioners in Advertising

A BAD GRAIN OF RICE

I hated my Dad.

I did not hate my Dad because he rationed my sugar addiction;
nor because he countered ad industry seduction of my tiny mind.
I did not hate my Dad because he beat me or abused me
(he was a loving, caring father who did neither).
I hated my Dad because he was Black.

My brother and I,
two Sri Lankan brothers up the street,
one brown-skinned boy (parentage unknown)
all went to a White school.

Teachers: White.
Playschool, cub-scouts, church, Sunday school: White.
Closest friends: White. Mother: White.
Dad: Black.

Dad at the school gates, parent's evening, sports day
reminding me I am not White.
Me. Shirking down into my parka-coat,
away from his proud beaming Black face.

Dad. So obvious. Chatting to other parents.
No thoughts for my embarrassment. No shame.
Kids. Staring. At him, at me. *Who's that?*
Is that his Dad? That's his Dad? Look how Black he is.

Dad.
Standing out amongst all the other normal faces.
A bad grain of rice in the dish.
Spoiling everything.

A grade A education. Fails.
A journey of name-calling, taunts,
patronising pats of Afro, scuffles, fights.
Self-application of clothes peg to reduce size of my nose.

Patient parents persist.
Journey to island in the sun, island of father's birth:
Great grandparents, favourite uncles, half-aunties,
second-cousins. Expanded horizons.

Daley Thompson and Viv my sports teachers.
Dreams to be like Mike – Jordan, Jackson, Tyson.
John Barnes, Bill Cosby, Mr T – big on black and white TV –
Beyond A Boundary to Mighty Gabby, Bob Marley, Muhammad Ali.

Journey towards being proud of my Dad,
being proud of who I am,
knowing who I am,
– a continuing extracurricular activity.

A love for difference slow-cooked:
an Afro pick for a silver spoon,
digging deep into cohobblopot of flying fish and cou cou.
Rice with spice. Flavoursome. Aromatic to the unpegged nose.

MAJORITY MONITORING

I am not ☐ Mixed-Race.

I am not ☐ Black or Black British:
Black African, Black Caribbean
or Any other Black background.

I am not ☐ White:
British, Irish or any other White background.

I am not ☐ Any other ethnic group.

I am not ☐ Other.

Depending on who is asking the question
what my mood is
how the question is asked
why the question is asked

I may be ☐ a Pomfretian-born Yorkshire writer of
Barbadian, English, Afrikan heritage.

I may be ☐ an artist, poet, designer, gardener, cook,
teacher, student, father, son, brother, lover.

I may be ☐ a revolutionary internationalist universalist
multiversalist Pan-Afrikan womanist
anarchist abolitionist activist.

Or not.

I would prefer
that this information was not used for monitoring purposes.

MY SON IS A TERRORIST

My son is a terrorist,
He's disturbing my peace.
My son is a terrorist,
I'm informing the police.

He looks like an Al Qaeda:
Beard needs a trim.
I read a terrorist profile,
Sounded just like him.

He criticises government,
Shouts at politicians on TV.
Brainwashed by fanatics:
No longer listens to me.

An ASBO is needed,
Quick, there isn't much time.
Bring in ID cards,
He's already plotting crime.

I don't know why he's angry
When poverty's gone for good,
We are addressing climate change
And we're giving Africa food.

My son is a terrorist,
Arrest him, clap him in chains.
He doesn't work alone,
And I can name names.

The ringleader may be Chomsky?
Klein? hooks? Pilger? Monbiot?
Each one preaches hatred
These instigators need to go.

They publish propaganda,
Distort the truth, tell lies,
A communist organisation
Calling explosion from the skies.

Dangerous, a mind of his own,
He could inspire others to think.
We live near a mosque –
That must surely be a link.

Please, arrest my son,
Tap phones, spy upon e-mail,
He's embarrassing his mother
He needs to be in jail.

Check his library records,
Take him away, erase his brain,
Return him like he used to be:
Sweet, innocent and sane.

Cuba's nice this time of year
Or darkest Uzbekistan,
Somewhere secret off the map
So as not to upset his Gran.

He needs to be reprogrammed.
Lock him up, make him see sense.
Install some patriotic values.
Torture him till he repents.

We used to watch Transformers,
Football with Des on Grandstand.
Please, bring back the boy I love,
He just doesn't understand.

MOVE, ME?

Maybe I should go back?
Back to where I come from? – "Get back!"
But most of my friends have moved away,
from Pontefract.

LOVE FOR LABOUR LOST

I picked you
the best of the bunch
Aroma of a New Dawn
Things could only get better

The prick of a thorn
Vision clears
I see you
for what you are:

Steel beneath soft rubber
Plastic painted petals
Serrated silicon leaves
Barbed wire branches

Your sweet smell sickens
Choking chemical perfume
Synthetic cyanide stink
A rose by focus group name

Vampire rose
Roots tunnelled in foreign lands
Rivers of blood to colour your head
I will not pick you again.

IV.

You can't trust politicians. It doesn't matter who makes a political speech. It's all lies – and it applies to any rock star who wants to make a political speech as well.

— Bob Geldof

RED TOPS

Metallic clatter of letter box:

Topless Evil Immigrant Paedophile
Sick slopped into cereal bowls

Celebrity Billionaire Cocaine WAG
Rumour spread on burnt toast

Insane Illegal Bomb Killer
Murder sipped with bitter coffee

Violent Asylum Gypsy Hoody
Yob sandwiched between white bread

Shock Horror Tragic Panic
Outrage sliced into neat triangles

Sexy Gay Cheating Pregnant
Terrorist sealed in Tupperware tubs

A repeat prescription: one tabloid a day…

ROCK, SCISSORS, PAPER

Scissors slice paper to reveal
the rock on which we stand.
On connection with rock,
rusted blades are sharpened.

The future forecasts storms.

Paper becomes transparent tissue:
lies wear thin, poison ink dilutes.
In centuries the rock will remain.
Scissors, drawn together, may survive.

NO IFS, NO BUTS

It lives in us all
One cut too deep, it rises
Blood. Revolution

ONE PERCENT EMPTY

Keys, ignition, accelerate.

And with that plan comes
bumping, crunching
over bodies, speeding
home to soak away the desert
in a champagne bubble bath.

Keys, ignition, splutter.
Splutter.

No gas.
No oil.
No power.

Through reinforced windows
glimpse
a change in the weather.

A rain of riot-stones.

SINQUEEN

— on the occasion of Elizabeth Windsor's 60 year reign as un-elected monarch

Reign reign
Off (with) your heads
Celebrate subjection
Sing. Dance. Wave flags in surrender.
Wave slaves.

SEVEN SEVEN

Seven times Seven brides for Seven Brothas
Seven Seven widows severed at Seven Sisters
Missed us. Whisprs — *they create clones uknow?*
How many hypntzd eyez comin outta Gntanmo?
9/11 lies, 7/7 disguise, CIA, MI6, MI5...
7x7, add 4+9, rcognze powah thrteen
Septmus Sever-us. Until Ubuntu. Uhuru. Afrikan dream.

SAVED BY SHOPPING

– inspired by and dedicated to (PRODUCT) RED™ : "the coming together of the distinct worlds of Africa and consumerism", "The Ideals of celebration and empowerment [which] doesn't rely on negative images or guilt driven participation" and "the joy that bringing two such tangibly different worlds together can create" (www.joinred.com)

deer
santa
i woud realy like
a afrikan baby
like brad and anjelina has
and maddonna
but just for weekends
as im still at scool
a boy wud be best
and i like the fat bellys
but no flys pleese
if yoo dont have any african babys left
then an i pod would be ok with tv and films on it
and woud be good to buy me becos
if you get a red one wich is my favorit color
bono from u2 and gizell who is ~~gore~~ ~~gorg~~ gorjus
will stop afrikan aids whitch is really bad
you coud also get me a red motorola mobile with tv and video messages
and other stuff too like an armarni watch converse sneakers and gap clothing
but i wouldent be allowd the red american express card until i am older
i have been good this yeer and ive started to eat brokerly
and i bought two wite braselets to make poverty history
mery xmas
love from
simon
xxxxxx
xxxxxx
xxxxxx

45

SICK JOKES

Q) Why did the celebrity cross the Channel?

A) To get their diseased fame-fixated soul out of the pit of self-loathing across to the other side of the green zone to bathe in the false beatifying light of charity before heading back to the gated green room to enjoy the consumption and lifestyle comforts that ensure the majority world remains impoverished and in apparent need of their once a year charitable stunts.

Q) What do you get if you cross several million petrochemical made-in-China red noses with a hyped-up dumbed-down UK population?

A) The end to World Poverty and Global Equality.

CONGOLESE COLLECT CALL

3, 010, 840

We are sorry
the DRC number you have dialled
is no longer in current use.
Please check and try again.

5, 020, 220

We are sorry
the number you have dialled
has not been recognised.
Please check and try again.

7, 560, 910

We are sorry
the number dialled is not valid
for UK, US and European networks.
Please check and try again.

9, 210, 630

We are sorry
but we are currently unable
to find a connection.
Please replace your handset,
Please replace your handset,
Please replace…

I MARINATED A MONSTER FROM OUT OF A SUPERMARKET FREEZER

— inspired by the John Cooper Clarke poems:
"I Married a Monster from Outer Space" and "Evidently Chicken Town"

A six foot genetically modified chicken
Too big for the supermarket shelf
A bargain at £3.99
Stuffed chicken – stuff my health

Bigger breasts than Jordan
Cheaper than Katie Price
I'll serve it with a parachute papadum
On a King-size bed of rice – nice

The best before date was yesterday
But we're living in a credit crunch
Chicken tonight, chicken tonight
And every night for a month – plus lunch

I wheel it home in a shopping trolley
Wouldn't fit in my car
200 pounds of naked bird
Lucky my house isn't far

Four hours on the floor to defrost
Even then it's tough as lead
Breaks every knife in the kitchen
I fetch the hedge-trimmer from the shed

I plug in the strimmer
The engine roars
My jerked chicken starts jerking
I'm sure it twitched its claws…

A head pops out the neck cavity
Shhhpop! – transgenic mutoid freak!
It tries to peck my pecker
Grabs my genitals with its beak

Foul play! Foul fowl!
Foul cock clucking at my crotch
I'll batter this bird-brained battery bantam
Stop it! Chop it on my chopping block

It jumps off the table
Rears up on Roberto Carlos thighs
It's bigger than Bernard Matthews
Round about Bernard Manning size

It slaps my face with a stubby wing
Chick chick chick-en! Cluck cluck!
Nobody but nobody calls me "chicken"
This hard-ass carcass is pushing its luck

I bash it with a saucepan
Again and again to tenderise
Garlic and paprika up its ass
Lemon juice and chilli in its eyes

I crack its wishbone, wring its neck
Kick its egg-sack for six – (that's a half dozen)
Hedge-trimmer off its wings – zzzum zzzum
And bung 'em in the oven

I skewer its leg with a pitchfork
It comes away at the bone
Aiming for its giblets
I drive the pitchfork home

The monster's on the ropes
So I truss it up quick
Strimmer off its other leg – zzzum zzzum
Knock it out with its own drumstick

The kitchen table makes a bonfire
A hundred litre soup in the bath
I'm hungry after the battle
I could eat a horse, mutant chicken or giraffe

The cooked bird is luminous green
When two hours later I check the clock
Smells like sweaty sewage
A bucket more Oxo in the stock

The "meat" has a plastic texture
I chew, I chew, aaaah-choo!
Rubbery flesh tastes of nothing:
Salmonella, SARS, hint of bird flu

I marinated a monster from a supermarket freezer
But I couldn't keep it down
Pesticides, steroids, preservatives
Puked up all over the ground

I marinated a monster from a supermarket freezer
Thinking GM was safe and sound
Forensics came to analyse the leftovers:
"No evidence of chicken found"

No evidence of chicken found.

ICEBERG BABY

Yo Shell/BP – let's kick it

Iceberg melting melting
Iceberg melting

Alright stop, collaborate, make 'em listen
Ice melt with fossil fool invention
Climate chaos grabs a hold tightly
Flow like a monsoon daily and nightly

Will it ever stop? We best hope so!
Turn off Tesco's lights – let's grow!
To the extreme we'll all be labelled "vandal"
Death of democracy – light a candle.

Dance – go rush the guns that boom
Evolve brains with psilocybin mushroom
Deadly as dope – that's the TV melody
corporate news – the peoples' enemy

Turn it off, leave it off, better not wait
Better cut the bull, teach the kid's to play
Yes, there's a problem, yo we gotta solve it
Repair our planet before Big Oil destroys it

Iceberg melting melting
Iceberg melting

Now that the party is ending
Prices sky high, oil no longer pumpin'
Quick to the pump to the pump no faking
Cooking CO_2 like a pound of bacon

Burning it – are we thick? Simple?
Crazy not to heed warning symbols

Wear a hard-hat in this Armageddon tempo
Civilisation on a roll – no time to go solo

Pursue climate criminals till they stop stop
Bust way past left-wing head to the black block
The block is worldwide
Yo so continue to repatriate all Beachfront Avenues

Girls, boys: balaclavas, bikinis
redistribute wealth, smash Lamborghinis
Yes, there's a problem, yo we gotta solve it
Repair our planet before greed destroys it

Iceberg melting melting
Iceberg melting

Take heed 'cause I'm an ecological poet
Land under sea if we don't take over it
'Cos our lifestyle's a chemical spill
Unfeasible, unsustainable: bankers – pay yo' bills

Class war by the rich – hell of a concept
Makes it tight for humanity to survive this
Check the temperature gauge – so fast,
Politician say damn – oil is a drug, buy it by the gram

Keep our composure – let oil loose
Community, renewables – kick the juice
Yes, there is a problem, yo we gotta solve it
Repair our planet before consumerism destroys it

Iceberg melting melting
Iceberg melting (oh-oh) too warm, too warm
Iceberg melting too warm, too warm

Yo man, woman, child – let's get outta here
Word to Mother Gaia
Peace.

V.

All I am saying is that the Black people would at least have known they were dealing with an honestly growling wolf, rather than a fox who could have them half-digested before they even knew what was happening.

— Omowale El-Hajj Malik El-Shabazz (Malcolm X)

To the best campaign team ever assembled in the history of politics – you made this happen, and I am forever grateful.

— Barack Obama, Ad Age Marketer of the Year, 2008

The modern little red riding hood, reared on singing commercials, has no objections to being eaten by the wolf.

— Marshall McLuhan

The use of advertising to sell statesmen is the ultimate vulgarity.

— David Ogilvy

Should advertising be abolished?
I found it difficult to deal with this menacing suggestion,
because I am neither an economist nor a philosopher.
But at least I was able to point out that opinion is divided.

— David Ogilvy

AAAAAAAAAAAAAAAAAAARGHHHH!

AAAAAAAAAAAAAAAAArghhhh!—
bolish all
celebration, commotion,
promotion of the notion
that we are free,
de owner of de plantation
now owns de penitentiary

I hear voices:
a chemical grey voice
blaired out
from behind
a plastic bush:

> Asbo
> Tesco
> Gitmo
> Let's go
> Back to work
> Back to school
> No stopping
> Business as usual
> — Carry on shopping.

An organic green voice
spreads seeds
like
neglected weeds:

Aaaaaaaaaaaa-bolish
abomination of corporation
ruling over di nation.
i-pod, i-phone, i-home, i-clone,
i, i, i... me, me, me, me,

quicker cheaper contracts
cannot bring liberty,
turn off big brother,
see reality c—c—t—v
di owner of di plantation
spells apartheID with ID...

Chemical grey blaired
behind bush:

> Human rights
> Have gone wrong
> Political madness
> Has gone correct
> Seven Seven
> Nine Eleven
> Dates we cannot
> Easily forget.

Green spreads seeds
neglected weeds:

Aaaaaaaaaaaa-bolish
digital control
over mind, body, soul,
empty email
turn Facebook face to a book,
reclaim time and space
that MySpace took,
look up from the gutter,
dim stars of celebrity,
di owner of di plantation
media monopoly...

Blair Brown
Bush Barrack:

Free press
Free vote
Free market
Free trade
Everything under control
Don't ask where –
Or how – it's made.

Green spreads weeds
neglected seeds:

Aaaaaaaaaaaa-bolish de myth
of freedom granted
by philanthropist
free freedom fighting names
of CLR James,
Nkrumah, Nanny, Nehanda and a
thousand Dessalines;
stitch bullet-holes of history
and herstory to see
de owner of de plantation
CEO of military...

Brown Blair
oBama Bush
Kameron Klegg
BaracK IraK

Drone on, drone on
Brown skin. Burning Bush. Devil's Blair.
Brown skin. White house. Black death.
Brown Bomba oBama Bush

        Stick to the curriculum
        Stay on course
        Turn to the chapter

"Abolition
= Wilberforce".
Do not upset the sponsors
No, it's not hypocritical
Feel free to speak freely
Just make sure it's not
Po-lit-i-cal.

Aaaaaaaaaaaa-bolish
media monopoly, ID, military,
abolish bomb-making nations,
abolish kkkorporations,
abolish the penitentiary
and — to be truly free,
abolish plantation owners
of de e-K-K-K-onomy.

Green weeds spread seeds

PRIDE OF BARBADOS

The Plantation™:
Will entertain with steel pan, stiltmen, fire-eaters, limbo and live music!
Will transport you (air-conditioned) from, and back to, your hotel
Will feed you, with an award-winning buffet
Will serve you free drinks – *all night long!*
The Plantation™ accepts all major credit cards.

The Plantation™:
Has its own website
Has a twenty-minute film informing of exciting ways to boost
the economy with your tax-free foreign currency
The Plantation™ pays at least the minimum wage.

The Plantation™:
Is sponsored by:
Mount Gay Rum – *the Island's oldest!*
Banks Beer – *exactly!*™
Colombian Emeralds – *Paradise in every box*™

The Plantation™:
Is a world-renowned showcase
Is a premier tourist attraction
Is featured on CNN, BET and major UK TV

The Plantation™:
Will be televised
Will be televised
Will be televised
And The Plantation™ is *always excellent!*™

REPARATION SONG

for sister Ekua, brother Mawukofi, Robert Nesta Marley

INTRO:
Wilberforce was the White saviour,
All Afrikans are dumb di dumb dumb

Old private trans-national corporations, yes, they still rob i;
Sold I Wilberwash and "heroes" like William Pitt,
Centuries after they supposedly freed i
We still dealing with destruction of we culture – identities –
institutions – societies – religions – philosophies – land –
peoples – history – herstory
and Black inferiority/ White supremacist bull-shit.

But my Haitian brothers and sisters – together with
Maroon uprisings – Afrikan resistance – and European
working-class solidarity movements – were strong
by repelling the armies of Spain, Napoleon and Blighty.
They died for this generation,
rebelling triumphantly.

So,
won't you help to bring
some movement towards holistic self-repairs
– societal change – global healing –
and eventual freedom?

'Cause we all need to have:

Reparations dialogue,
Reparations dialogue.

Do not congratulate yourselves for abolition of slavery;
When kkkapitalism still capture we body and mind.
Wo! Pay no tax for atomic weapon or energy,
'Cause all-o-dem is just-a climate crime.
For long must we kill their profits,
Till they stand aside and look?
The human race, yes, we're all a part of it:
They got to give-a-back what dey took.

So,
won't you help to bring
dese first steps in the process of global justice – truth
– reconciliation – and overstanding the complexities and
legacies of Maangamizi (the Afrikan holocaust of
chattel – colonial – and neo-colonial – enslavement)
and true freedom?

'Cause we all need to have:

Reparations dialogue
Reparations dialogue
Reparations dialogue.

THE C WORD

as we move onwards ever upwards,
forwards never backwards
we see words, we say words,
hear words, connect words

C words: culture carbon climate change,
overused words, abused words
deliberately confused words
by one unspoken silent C word

C – supporter of conservative, labour,
liberal, republican, democratic governments
C behind all criminal cartel corrupt corporate...

                                        stunts

mr newsreader, mr newswriter,
cultural commentator, master debater
be brave, no longer fear the client
let this C word no longer be silent

Columbus, Churchill, church colonise.
conquer, cut, crusade civilise.
coerce, corrode, consume Coca

                        Cola.

mother earth – we have identified your would be assassin
we know the enemy's shame
this poem has been brought to you by:
the countless number slain

and the letter C.
let us speak the devil's name
free ourselves from prison:
cuh... cah... cap... cap-it... capit-al...
KKKAPITALISM.

FULL CIRCLE

for Jane Trowell, Dorothea Smartt & the C Words Family

TINA: There Is No Alternative[*]
TABOO: There Are Billions Of Options

proposition I

enough words!
let us move forwards,
but let us look backwards
fly like Sankofa,
this world is for turning

full circle
back to nature,
back to origins,
back to Mama Afrika,
back to Mother Earth

connect
re-connect
to the womb-an
wombanise our world
re-capture, reclaim our words.

[*]Margaret Thatcher

proposition II

know yourself
know the ledge
test the edges
embrace taboo
utter: "cunt"

reclaim cunt from cokkks
never mind the bollocks
literal, critical, clitoral
clit on tongue tips
cunning linguists, vagina dialogue

ja, ihr könnt
– yes, you can
ken, kenne, können,
knowledge, power, womb-an,
connection, ya ken?

proposition III

let the Iron Lady rust
seed bomb the car-cass
kill TINA,
embrace TABOO:

trust power of populations
over Optimum Population Trusts
power to produce
re-duce
re-distribute.

open borders, open minds,
eat forbidden foraged fruit
touch the exhibits
write back at the madness that surrounds,
break down the Palace walls.

proposition IV

comrades, citizens, co-operatives,
come create community — co-mutiny
cross-cultural, cross-continental connection,
communicating controversial conversation.

critical-mass convivial consensus,
cultivating, constructing, campaigning,
cooking, clowning, climate-camping,
co-operating, collaborating, co-realizing.

realize, re-member, re-connect
resistance, remembrance, repairs
we come full circle.
come together, come as we are
radical in our natural beauty.

come

      cunts
          cocks

              cuddle.

THIRD LIFE LESSONS

Rush hour. Speed down Chapeltown Road.
Car slows.

Options: crash into, crash over, crash under,
fall before.

Screech of cycle brakes, no helmet:
Option four.

Rucksack of Young Authors tees saves back.
Thick dreads saves head.

Scraped elbow, knocked knee, gouged shin.
Still breathing.

Curse car. Recover bottle, frame and dignity.
Late to workshop – trust games.

Next day, discover broken wrist – a lesson:
Slow down. Breathe. Stop.

Breathing. A blessing.

BIRTHING SPACE

for Kinsi Abdulleh & the NUMBI family

Datelines cut / Thirteen menstrual moons sliced
into twelve forced labours. Caesarian sections.

Caesar dictates / Forceps. Gas. Air.
Pupils dilated, students splayed, pepper-sprayed.

Snot streams / Black soot bogies bring salt water
remembrance of our trans-Atlantic traffic.

Oil exhausts / Inhale carboniferous ancestors:
Bubbles of resistance to oxygenate the brain.

Escape toxi-city / Open the gate to a rich mix,
A Numbi healing. Dance. Sing. Breathe.

Rise. Up / Join global, local, voices.
And breathe. And breathe. And breathe.

NECESSARY FREEDOMS

for Jayne Cortez

In answering a poetic task set by Sister Cortez he recounts his
admiration for Brother Malcolm and Sister Nawaal.

In contemplating the true essence of freedom he asks himself
how free can we truly be? Can we be so true to self that we

forget self? Forget who we are supposed to be, and just be? Free.
Naked when all others are clothed? Sit, while others stand?

Stand, while others sit? Dancing to the beat of our heart. So
fucking free to scream, to shout, without consequence, without

conscience? To cry, and not know, not care, why. Laughing for
the beauty, for the futility of it all. Om........................

He meditates on Malcolm… olm. Om. Omowale El-Haajj Malik El-
Shabazz. Yes, being once already dead one can truly live without

fear of death. He renounces his name and gender. He/she
becomes they. Then they want for nothing. They leave the

washing up to eat from the earth, from out of the bins. They
ponder barefoot under great acacias in northern forests, roam

bare-chested across southern plains, making love, as and when.
They wonder about the question: is this freedom or has the ego

just exchanged itself for self indulgence? To be free like El Saadawi
causes consternation. At eighty years young, maybe they too will

be on the front lines, but to be free from all worry for family is
perhaps to be too free? Troubled by unreconciled urges, the

nagging pang of revolution, faith, duty and surrounded by nonbelievers
he returns to change nappies and dig vegetables, home.

REVELATIONS

In the end there will be the word.
The word of the inner God beyond flesh.
Perfect combinations:
inner God + inner Goddess.

The image + the word. The dream.
+ the sound + taste + smell + feel + the sixth,
seventh, intuitive natural infinite ingrained
telepathic, telekinetic, one-consciousness sense.

This word is all.
Alpha. Omega.
A. Z.
Om. Ahhh.

Ageless. Aboriginal.
Adinkra. Alkebulan.
Akoben. Akoma.
Asase ye duru. One.

This, the word of your inner God/inner Goddess.
For Ours is the Kingdom/Queendom.
Shared power, all glory.
Forever and ever,

Amen-ra.
A(womb)en.
Amenyana.
Ashe.

ABOUT THE AUTHOR

Sai Murray is a poet, author, spoken word artist, graphic artist of Bajan/ Afrikan/ English descent. The first part of his debut novel, *Kill Myself Now: The True Confessions of an Advertising Genius* is published by Peepal Tree Press.

Sai is politics and culture editor of *SABLE LitMag*; artistic director of *Scarf magazine*; and the editor of the anthologies: *Re-Membering – A Creative Journey to Wholeness*, Artists in Mind (AiM); *No Condition Is Permanent* (Platform); *The Write Stuff #1-3* (AiM). In 2009 he was commissioned as one of two poets for Platform's C Words project and was chosen as one of Yorkshire's eight most talented literary/ visual artists for *FWords: Creative Freedom* (2008).

Sai is a resident poet at Numbi, a member of the digital artists collective Virtual Migrants, and he collaborates regularly with international musicians across genres (including DJ Eric Soul, Chris Campbell and members of Nneka's band, Bronzehead).

He is a founding poet/facilitator on Platform's youth arts and activism project, *Shake!* and has coached teams to victory in the 2009, 2010, 2012 Voices of a New Generation Slam, the GSAL Speak Up Slam 2012, and at the largest ever UK national slam, Shake the Dust. Sai currently works as a mentor and runs creative writing workshops for the mental health arts charity, AiM.

As creative director of Liquorice Fish, Sai publishes, designs and contributes artwork for a number of grassroots community organisations.

PRAISE FOR AD-LIBERATION:

Dynamic, but also very subtle. Comic wordplay runs throughout this volume, but Sai uses it to build a picture of a complex web of interrelationships – how racism works with capitalism, how legacies of empire live on, how the manipulative language of mass media seeks our souls, how our planet's ecology is inseparable from social justice, how poetry and poetics can change the story, how individual experience forms consciousness. But also, the poems use human everyday life: what it's like to perform to three people, or have a near miss falling off your bike. Or, to make sense of acutely shameful feelings about how white people see your black father. By richly interleaving the personal and fallible with the dramatic and the political, the anthology doesn't fall into the traps which can be common pitfalls for activist art. Like preaching to the converted, or "whatever it is, we're against it" oppositionalism. You won't find bland propagandistic aesthetics here – Sai employs many techniques and each page delights with new tastes

At heart, *Ad-Liberation* is deadly serious. Sai Murray's poetry reveals a hunger for change. This volume nourishes the hunger we have, but more importantly reveals the hunger we didn't know we were suffering from.

— *Red Pepper* magazine

Exploratory, original and engaged...
— Robert Newman, political comedian/ author

A linguistic energy which is potent both in performance and on the page
— Caryl Phillips, author of *Foreigners*

A truly original voice
— Courttia Newland, author of *Snakeskin*